DISSOLVE THE PAST

*Finishing Your Incomplete
Act of Escape*

ROBBIE GRAYSON III

©Robert W. Grayson III
All rights reserved.
2024

No part of this book may be used or reproduced by any means: graphic, electronic, or mechanical, including photocopying, recording, taping, or by any information storage retrieval system without the written permission of the author except in the case of brief quotations embodied in critical articles and reviews. Because of the dynamic nature of the Internet, any web addresses or links contained in this book may have changed since publication and may no longer be valid. Although every precaution has been taken to verify the accuracy of the information contained herein, the author and publisher assume no responsibility for any errors or omissions, so that no liability is assumed for damages that may result from the use of information contained within. The views expressed in this work are solely those of the author and do not necessarily reflect the views of the publisher whereby the publisher, hereby disclaims any responsibility for them.

ATTRIBUTIONS
Interior Text Font: Minion Pro
Cover Design & Typesetting: Robbie Grayson III
Additional Credits on Credits Page

BOOK PUBLISHER INFORMATION
A Division of Traitmarker Media, LLC
www.traitmarkerbooks.com
traitmarker@gmail.com

ISBN: 979-8-8691-6591-6

Printed in the United States of America

Table of Contents

A Note from the Publisher (iv)

Preface (v)

I. Intro: Time | 11

II. Psychological Time | 28

III. Natural Time | 42

IV. The Triune Brain | 60

V. Energy | 78

VI. Freeze & Discharge | 91

VII. Dissolve the Past | 118

Credits | 138

Quotes | 140

About the Author

A NOTE
FROM THE PUBLISHER

The publisher is providing this book and its contents on an "as is" basis and makes no representations or warranties of any kind with respect to this book or its contents and disclaims all such representations and warranties, including but not limited to warranties of mental healthcare for a particular purpose.

The content of this book is for informational purposes only and is not intended to diagnose, treat, cure, or prevent any mental condition or disease. This book is not intended as a substitute for consultation with a licensed practitioner. Please consult with a physician or healthcare specialist regarding the suggestions and recommendations made in this book.

TRAITMARKER MEDIA, LLC

The Purpose of This Book

I burned all of my journals a few years ago. The entries spanned the late 1980s through 2016. People were revolted when I mentioned it.

"Why would you do that?" they asked.

I should have kept my mouth shut because, at the time, I didn't even understand it myself.

Almost dying in May 2016 changed my mind about keeping those little notebooks in which I had committed my cleverest musings for thirty-plus years. In short, I learned that my decades-long habit of reflective journaling was a key mechanism preventing me from overcoming signature holding patterns because it was procrastination disguised as "doing something."

Previously, when I would hit a resilience roadblock and a situation crippled me, I would retreat to my attic and reverently pull out my journals, consulting them like a Ouija board. What was I looking for? I was looking for the "key" to getting over myself that, once discovered, would make sense of my loneliness, anger, anxiety, or whatever Achilles heel I found myself nursing at the time. And I believed the key was somehow encoded in the overabundance of what I had written in those notebooks.

But each time I would read a journal entry, I would be pulled down memory rabbit holes where the siren song of nostalgia distracted me from the trouble at hand. And if I lingered long enough, I would be rewarded with a dopamine rush of wistfulness indistinguishable from salvation.

And when I left the garage? I was actually worse off than when I went in. When I went into the attic, at least I knew I needed to *do* something. But when I came out, I would be under the hypnotic spell of what psychologists call *dissociation*.

But when I almost died in May 2016, something changed. One minute, I had defaulted to the attic once again to spread my notebooks across the attic floor. The next minute, I understood that I was to burn them all.

So, I set all of them on fire. When the

chimnea on my front porch couldn't handle the workload, I started a second fire in the backyard firepit—two fires burning at once. The ashes smoldered for the better part of two days, and the smoke hovered over the property twice as long.

The next day, I could see the haze eerily distorting the skyline around my house—like ghosts reluctant to leave. But when it finally lifted, I felt free.

But, again, why did I do it? That's what this little book is about.

ROBBIE GRAYSON III
Franklin, Tennessee | January 2024

You can't have a better past.
RICHARD CARLSON

intro
time

In grade school, we were taught that three tenses make up time:

1) past
2) present
3) future

Each tense required us to focus on time in different ways:

1) The past required us to *remember*
2) The present requires us to *do*
3) The future will require us to *want*

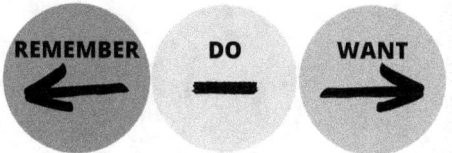

Dissolve the Past

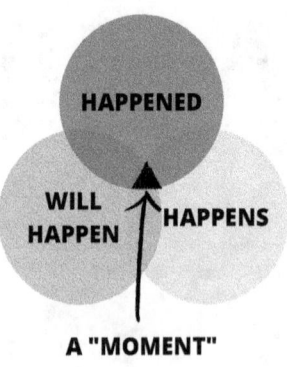

We learned to blend all three tenses into the smallest unit of time. I'll call it a *moment:*

1) what *happened*
2) what *happens*
3) what *will happen*

DISSOLVE THE PAST

With this mindset,
how much of a *moment*
does each tense get?

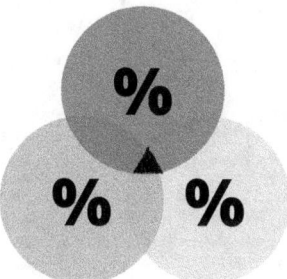

DISSOLVE THE PAST

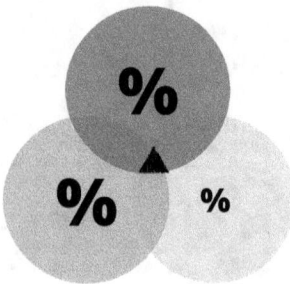

Whatever the actual percentages, the *present* gets the *lowest*. Why? Because it's the only tense in which we *do* anything.

When you *take* a photo, that's kinetic energy. It's the *present*.

Once you *complete the act of taking the photo*, it's spent energy. It's the *past*.

If you *want* to take a photo, it's potential energy that isn't spent and hasn't yet become kinetic. It's *future*.

Robbie Grayson III

DISSOLVE THE PAST

PAST   **PRESENT**   **FUTURE**

Having taken the photo (past) and *not yet taking the photo* (future) aren't equal in energy to *taking* the photo. *Remembering* and *wanting* energies are imagined because neither is equal to or greater than the act of *doing.*

Doing energy operates on a different channel frequency than *remembering* and *wanting* energies. Not being kinetic, the past and future are *psychological* energies. You can *think* about *remembering* and *wanting,* but by thinking you *do* nothing about either.

PAST   **PRESENT**   **FUTURE**

Dissolve the Past

You can't *do* anything with the full power the *present* affords if you share it with *remembering* and *wanting*. If, however, you believe you can, then the "present" gets the lowest percentage of a "moment."

That's what this little book is about.

Stress is a sign that you've lost the present moment. The next moment has become more important than life itself.

ECKHART TOLLE

ii
psychological time

Blending past, present, and future into a moment is *psychological time*. *Psychological time* is best summed up as *a lifestyle characterized by always being behind.*

Robbie Grayson III

DISSOLVE THE PAST

It isn't possible for you to think *about* the present, because the present is kinetic energy happening *now*.

However, it's possible for you to think *in* the present, because the present is the only time in which you *do* anything.

Thinking *about* the present is a psychological convention given equal or more weight than doing *in* the present. "Borrowing" against the present like this, psychological time creates a space entirely reserved for re-experiencing the past. Thinking *about* the present becomes an added step to *doing* in the present.

Robbie Grayson III

Dissolve the Past

By thinking *about* the present, psychological time creates a delay between *thinking* and *doing*. When you live in the present this way, you forfeit the full power of *doing*. That might not seem like a big deal at first, but the micro-delays stack up as a result until you experience the paralysis of *anxiety.*

Psychological time constantly interrupts us from *doing* fully in exchange for *thinking-not-doing*. By *doing*, we use the body. By *thinking-not-doing*, we use the mind.

Doing is like putting your foot on the accelerator of a car—there's no delay between the intention and the act.

Thinking-not-doing is like putting one foot on the accelerator *while* putting the other foot on the brake. A lot of energy is generated, but the car goes nowhere. The intention results in immobility.

Robbie Grayson III

DISSOLVE THE PAST

Psychological time values *thinking-not-doing* over *doing*, even though *thinking-not-doing* results in delay—its worst feature. How does it make up for delay? By requiring you to increase effort, which also means increasing more *thinking-not-doing!*

But no matter how much you increase effort, by psychological time's design, you are *always* behind.

So, by increasing more *thinking-not-doing*, you are proportionately doing less. At some point, the accumulation of little delays becomes disruptive and eventually fatal to your efforts to do anything on time.

That's the trap of psychological time. And that's what this little book is about.

*The first rule is to keep an untroubled spirit.
The second is to look things in the face and
know them for what they are.*

MARCUS AURELIUS

iii
natural time

The backdrop to psychological time is natural time. Natural time is like a container for everything in our universe. Psychological time, like everything else in our universe, is a *thing* as well and fits inside that container.

NATURAL TIME

DISSOLVE THE PAST

If natural time were a computer operating system, then psychological time would be the software. In order for the software to work, it needs to be compatible with the operating system. The software doesn't have to be optimal for the operating system to run it. It could work—more or less—by running fast or slow or by glitching or freezing.

Think about walking across the floor wherever you are. Done? Now *actually* do it.

Do you *feel* the difference?

Psychological time abstracts natural time by *thinking* about it. Natural time isn't abstract—it is what it is *now*.

ROBBIE GRAYSON III

Dissolve the Past

Natural time is a better reference than psychological time for fitting yourself into the way things work. That's because psychological time exists nowhere in the universe but in your head. Natural time influences everything in our universe.

Natural time says, *This is how it is.*

Psychological time says, *This is how I think it should be.*

If natural time had a language, it would be the cycle. You can learn a lot about a cycle by "listening" to it:

- First, watch one rotation.
- Second, watch another.
- Third, watch several in a row.
- Fourth, watch several in different situations.

To learn the vocabulary of a cycle, you first must experience how that cycle repeats itself. When you experience a cycle enough times, you begin to "hear" it talk to you.

Robbie Grayson III

Dissolve the Past

You experience a cycle best when you're present to it. You experience a cycle least when you think about it.

Before being potty trained, you initially weren't aware of your biology in a way you could control it. However, you increasingly become aware of the discomfort. During potty training, you became more acutely aware of the discomfort without the convenience of a dry diaper. You eventually got so good at "reading" your biology that you learned by experience to avoid accidents altogether.

What allowed you to "read" your biological cycle? Experience. What allowed you to avoid accidents? *Doing what was necessary to avoid the accident.* In other words, emotional intelligence.

Emotional intelligence is like an audio mixer. By sliding levers and turning knobs, you learn different combinations that *don't* work for the frequency you want until you discover the ones that get you closer to one you want. *Then* you discover the right one.

When we raise our emotional intelligence by listening to the cycles of which we are a part, we become more attuned to doing the thing that gives us the frequency we want.

Robbie Grayson III

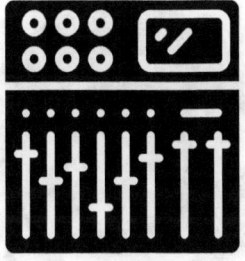

DISSOLVE THE PAST

Because psychological time requires delay, it isn't as efficient as natural time in reading cycles. By abstracting natural time into a thought about "how things should work," psychological time hampers your emotional intelligence from reaching its optimal peak.

By preferring psychological time, we must always be late, always be slow, and always be a little "off" instead of moving *at the right moment*.

But what happens when you increase your effort to make up for the accumulated delays of psychological time?

That's what the next chapter is about.

*Unfortunately for our
species, our cages are
often cultural and of
our own making.*

ROBERT SCAER

iv
the triune brain

The human brain integrates three important parts that work together to increase our emotional intelligence. They are as follows from darkest/lowest to lightest/highest:

3) *reptile* brain
2) *mammal* brain
1) *primate* brain

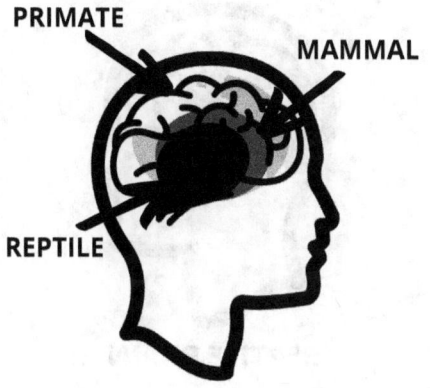

Dissolve the Past

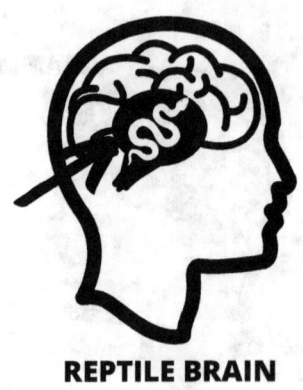

REPTILE BRAIN

The Reptile Brain

The reptile brain regulates involuntary survival drives like heartbeat, breath, hunger, thirst, spatial orientation, and the urge to self-defense. Key to these drives is its involuntary and "cold-blooded" nature, which means *they don't require a conscious thought to work.* You don't need a conscious thought to make your heart beat, be thirsty, or be hungry.

The Mammal Brain

The mammal brain works for reward and regulates behavior that supports your survival within a group. These traits are "warm-blooded," like negotiation, diplomacy, and the ability to discern rank. You can't get what you need to survive among competitors if you can't figure out the rules that get and/or keep you there.

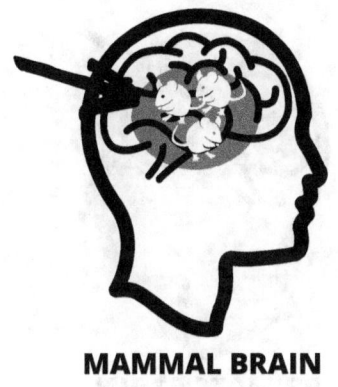

MAMMAL BRAIN

DISSOLVE THE PAST

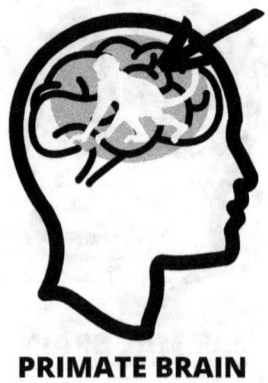

PRIMATE BRAIN

The Primate Brain

The finer parts of the neocortex make up the consciousness of the primate brain. Consciousness involves awareness and reflection of both inner and outer lives. These attributes deliberately use language, give motor commands, and sort out sensory perceptions. We can control thoughts in this area. That makes us able to pick and choose, mix and match, agree or disagree.

BRAIN INTEGRITY

Each part of the brain serves its own distinct role and works in concert with the others. The sum effect is what I call a "spiritual" mind. I don't mean a "religious" mind. A spiritual mind drives us to contribute beyond survival and gives us the means to do it by present *doing* power.

Robbie Grayson III

Dissolve the Past

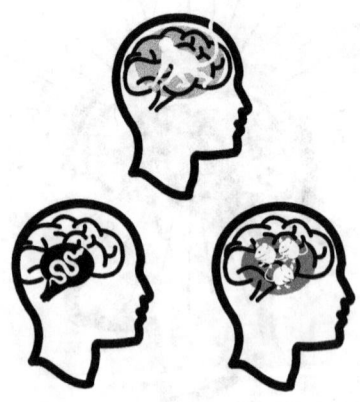

By emphasizing *thinking-not-doing* energy to be equal to or greater than *doing* energy, psychological time suppresses the concerted effort of the triune brain. By isolating the finer skills of the primate brain, it atrophies the integrity of the entire brain, which results in stymied emotional intelligence.

Mind-Body Language

If each region of the brain is an integration of parts and all three regions are an integrated whole, we can assume that each region mirrors the same unified message of the whole—each in its own way.

Key to learning a language is discovering the mechanism for translating each into the vocabulary of the other. Let's examine the languages of the primate and reptile brains.

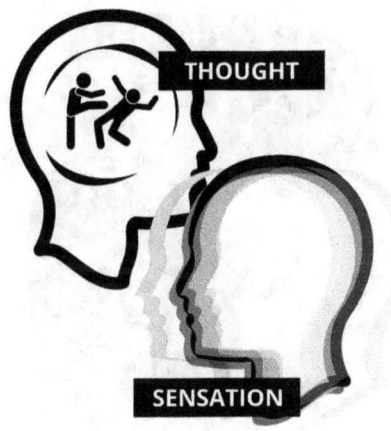

DISSOLVE THE PAST

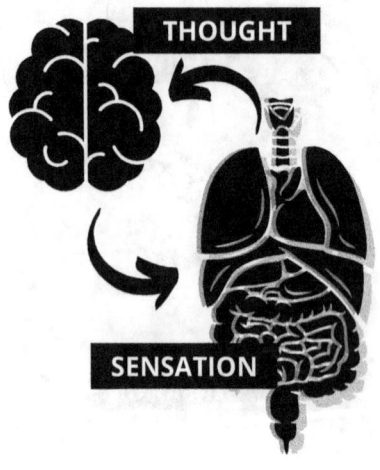

The primate brain speaks the language of *thought* in which memory is the psychological recollection of past events. This brain uses *psychological* energy. The reptile brain speaks the language of *behavior* in which memory is *also* the recollection of past events but in the form of *neurological* energy. So, not only is memory *thought*, but it's also *neurological sensation*.

When we speak about the past, we're usually referring to the "past tense," because we're thinking within the convention of psychological memory. When I use the word "past" from this point forward, I mean neurological memory, which is *any negative sensation happening in the body now.*

*People do not
decide their futures.
They decide their habits,
and their habits decide their futures.*

F.M. ALEXANDER

V
energy

Because there's a direct correlation from one form of memory to another, there's a direct correlation of thought to neurological sensation—even though you might be unconscious of it.

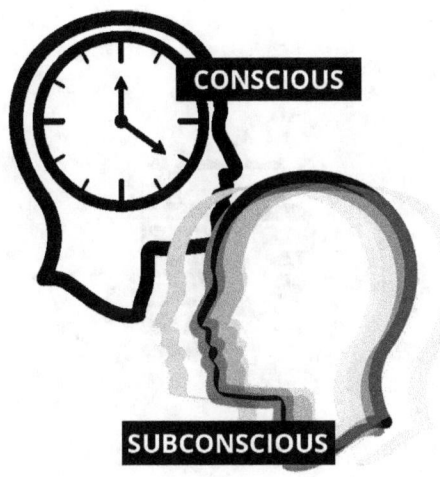

Dissolve the Past

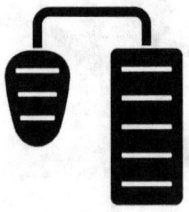

Because psychological time weakens *doing,* it causes a lag between the intention of the mind and the response of the body. But even though the mind bullies the body in this way, the body doesn't entirely concede because it's directly subject to natural time.

Here's where we see the frictional relationship between psyche and body. Both have a foot on the accelerator—and brake!

Because psychological time requires you to compulsively flex *thought* before *doing*, the reptile brain must wait for the primate brain 1) to ruminate and then 2) convert thought into action.

But by the time the body "gets" the signal the brain is giving it, the moment for acting has passed, and the action becomes irrelevant.

And what if your life were at stake?

DISSOLVE THE PAST

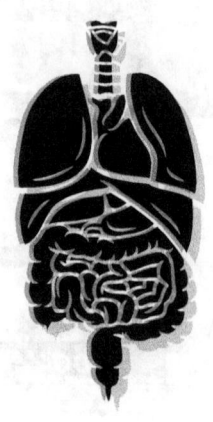

When you're sick, tired, upset, or in some sort of trouble, psychological time doesn't "hear" the signals that nature gives the body as they happen (the present) because its "perception frequency" is on a different channel (the past).

But the reptile brain is speaking in its own neurological language—blood pressure, hyperventilation, headaches, gut issues, sleep cycle disruptions, and other sensations.

Psychological time is only attuned to what it is conscious of and what it can control. Listening to behavioral memory isn't its priority because behavioral memory is unconscious. At the same time, natural law keeps sending signals to the reptile brain that largely go unread because psychological time runs a script to override it.

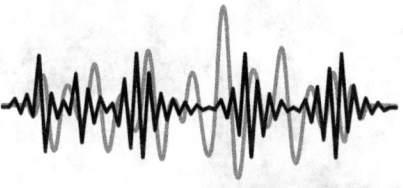

Dissolve the Past

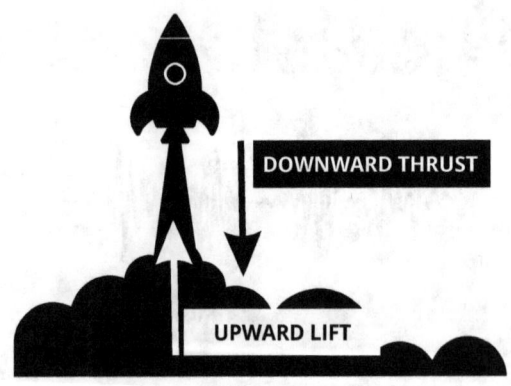

When the body isn't allowed to bring closure to a psychological thought, the energy generated (build-up) embeds itself within the nervous system because it has nowhere to go.

It's similar to a rocket launch. The thrust must be greater than the lift to launch the rocket successfully. If the build-up in the body were allowed to "discharge" at the moment of action, then the energy generated would be "used up" and pass through the system. This is natural.

The delays generated by psychological time express themselves as excess energy embedded within the nervous system. Because these delays accumulate and must go somewhere, the nervous system makes room for the excess energy through a series of short-circuit compensations like memory lapses, muscle spasms, involuntary tremors, nervous tics, etc.

Robbie Grayson III

Dissolve the Past

Fight, Flight, Freeze

A popular model of the energy generated in the face of threat is the fight, flight, and freeze model.

- FIGHT: The individual "closes in" on the threat to extinguish it.

- FLIGHT: The individual "puts distance" between themselves and the threat in order to evade it.

- FREEZE: The individual is unable to move.

According to this model, the only two viable options for successfully escaping a threat are to fight or flee. The freeze is described as an involuntary act outside one's control.

Because nature isn't either-or, it provides a spectrum of unconscious energies:

- FIGHT (++): *The positive of the positive.* Expend energy by moving towards the threat with the intent to engage it.

- FEIGN (+-): *The negative of the positive.* Expend energy by moving towards the threat with no intent to engage it but with the hope it will go away.

- FAWN (--): *The negative of the negative.* Expend energy by making oneself as small a target as possible to avoid conflict.

- FLEE (-+): *The positive of the negative.* Expend energy by putting distance between oneself and the threat.

Dissolve the Past

The First Thing

When an animal senses that fighting is advantageous, it will engage the threat to eliminate it. If it senses that putting distance between itself and the better option, then that works just as well. Fawning (e.g., playing dead) and feigning (e.g., arching back) also work in certain situations. Biologically, *whichever tactic works in a situation is the correct one* because it ends up being the effective one.

The animal that successfully extinguishes a threat does so by using energy it builds up in the face of that threat.

Whatever excess energy is left over, the animal will work it out of its nervous system. Some animals involuntarily shake, while others remain hyper-vigilant until the nervous system returns to homeostasis.

Once the animal's nervous system reaches homeostasis, it has discharged all extra energy and is no longer in a triggered state. The only purpose of excess energy is to support the excess effort needed to escape a threat.

Dissolve the Past

The Second Thing

The correct response to an immediate threat is *always* behavioral, not psychological. Consulting a thought before *doing* more than likely will result in a failed attempt at escape because your response will be delayed by the time the threat envelopes you.

"Staying in your head" during the moment of action numbs the physical sensation of the failed attempt and embeds the excess energy in your behavioral memory. And you will be none the wiser—even when it ties you up in inexplicable holding patterns or erupts in unpredictable outbursts. And who knows what innocent "triggers" will call this memory out of your body, disrupting your life again and again? This is the *past*.

But it's not "out" there somewhere. It's "in" you.

What about freezing? If it's not a conscious escape option, then what is it?

That's what the next chapter is about.

*We do
not suffer
by accident.*

JANE AUSTEN

vi
freeze & discharge

There are times during an escape attempt when the energy that is built up in the face of threat doesn't discharge in a successful escape. The result is *freezing*.

Dissolve the Past

Freezing is often misunderstood as a choice instead of an involuntary response when it's actually an interruption *during* the act of escape. In other words, the individual was *in the act of* fighting, fleeing, feigning, or fawning *when* the interruption occurred.

A group of biologists in a helicopter were trailing a polar bear to tranquilize and tag it. The polar bear, an apex predator, instinctively chooses to flee the threat by running away. Unsuccessful, the bear is tranquilized and immobilized.

There are three important factors to learn from the polar bear's situation.

THREAT

The threat, being above and beyond, makes it **omnipresent**, so impossible to fight.

FLIGHT

The instinct of the polar bear is to flee the omnipresent threat as a viable escape tactic.

Dissolve the Past

Escape Option: Flight

First, the polar bear chooses the option of flight:

- FIGHTING is not an option. The threat, being "above and beyond," is out of reach.

- FEIGNING is not an option. The threat, being "higher and larger," is more ominous than the polar bear.

- FAWNING is not an option. The bear is an apex predator and unfamiliar with the ritual of submission.

Therefore, the polar bear instinctively chooses flight.

Dissolve the Past

Freeze & Collapse

Second, the polar bear's flight is interrupted because it's tranquilized. How the polar bear is immobilized is of no importance to it because the interruption is a "near-death" (or "near-as-death") experience.

The polar bear then "collapses" into a neurologically helpless state called the freeze. It's misguided to assume that because the polar bear is immobile, it has stopped "running" altogether. Remember the illustration of the brake and accelerator. When the feet are on the accelerator and brake at the same time, the engine generates a lot of energy but goes nowhere.

So, while the bear is immobilized, there's a build-up of energy with nowhere for it to go.

COLLAPSE

The polar bear is interrrupted midrun and collapses. We call this "freezing," but the polar bear is *still* trying to escape.

Dissolve the Past

DISCHARGE

As the polar bear **discharges the freeze,** it completes the act of escape (running) until its nervous system expels all excess energy generated in the build-up.

Third, as the polar bear begins to move, it appears to have a seizure. But if you look carefully, it isn't a seizure, per se—the bear is "running" in an involuntary, erratic way, though going nowhere. What does this mean?

The polar bear is neurologically completing the act of escape. Because it was interrupted mid-run, it discharges excess energy by completing the run. But why now? Because the intelligence of its reptile brain senses that it *no longer needs the excess energy it generated in the face of the threat.*

When the polar bear comes out of the freeze completely, it might be exhausted and wiser for the encounter, but what it *won't be* is burdened with excess energy bound up in its nervous system, provoking it at arbitrary times to break out into a run for its life to its own confusion.

Even though discharging the freeze sounds simplified for wild animals, it works similarly for humans—but with an important caveat. Wild animals are directly attuned to their natural environments, which puts them in direct contact with natural time. Civilized people, however, are more directly attuned to civilized sensibilities like psychological time. The barriers that prevent humans from discharging the freeze are ideological, but the freeze isn't discharged psychologically. It's discharged neurologically.

So long as humans insist on the superiority of psychological time over natural time, the past will bury itself deep within our nervous system, bore itself deep into our organs, hijacking our pulse and our blood. It will hound us until our dying day. And in the end, we will call it bad luck, a spiritual attack, or destiny.

*The resistance to the
unpleasant situation is
the root of suffering.*

RAM DASS

vii
dissolve the past

Whatever one's opinion is, avoiding injury or death in the face of a threat *isn't* the final aim of escape. If avoidance is the aim, then the escape hasn't been completed, and the threat hasn't entirely been extinguished.

Homeostasis is what completes the act of escape.

Robbie Grayson III

Dissolve the Past

Mainstream confusion over what constitutes a freeze is largely responsible for how we understand and construct stories that popularize the incomplete act of escape. That story trope is of the superhero with a traumatic past they have overcome—the *origin* story. But years later, out of nowhere, the traumatic event comes back to haunt them in the form of a new enemy.

We use this same framework to share our own experiences—a framework in which we admire survivors of bad childhoods, physical assault, bankruptcy, war, or divorce who each chose to escape by fight or flight. We admire them because we assume they didn't choose the third option—freeze.

But then we come to expect that the threat they escaped comes back to haunt them. Why?

Because *escaping* and *extinguishing the threat* are two different things.

Freezing isn't a psychological choice—it's a biological response to the feeling of overwhelm in the face of threat—*even if one fights or flees.*

The individual who doesn't discharge excess energy from the encounter—safe though they might be—still can be "stuck" *in* the act of fighting, fleeing, fawning, or feigning for years to come! This is the essence of the freeze. Consider the following examples.

DISSOLVE THE PAST

Robbie Grayson III

The Freeze in Submission

A woman experiences a series of bad romantic relationships. Each begins with strong physical attraction, dizzying emotional fulfillment, and a promise of fidelity but ends in physical abuse, betrayal, or both. At some point, she defaults to the following psychological reasoning:

Why does this always happen to me? What have I ever done to deserve this? Why can't someone be there for me like I'm there for them? I'll do things differently next time.

Though this woman escaped each destructive relationship, what she didn't do was physically discharge the freeze of submission. Submissive energy has become an unconscious cycle embedded in her behavioral memory. Her body literally scans her environment for situations that allow the excess energy of submission to find expression.

Dissolve the Past

The Freeze in Feigning

A man suffers from a chronic illness he's had for most of his life in which he was shielded by doting parents. He makes a series of public declarations that he will improve his situation by moving out on his own, looking to date, or launching a business. At the moment of decision, however, his plans get derailed *every* year by strange bouts of illness. His internal dialogue goes something like this:

Aha! I knew this would happen—again. I'll just have to wait until next year because things are going to get worse—again. It always happens like this—every time I'm about to do something huge.

Perhaps every applause he gets for expressing great intention generates the posturing cycle. He's unconsciously attracted to situations in which he is unable to follow through.

Robbie Grayson III

DISSOLVE THE PAST

The Freeze in Fighting

A military veteran transitions into the civilian world. Whether or not a combat veteran, they find themselves agitated when encountering "non-regulation" situations that cause them unnecessary delays, increase their confusion, and demonstrate arbitrary control over their freedom:

I'm not answering that question—that's none of your goddamn business. I'm not standing in line over there—ring me up over here, you lazy motherfucker. Show me your badge number. Show me the rule.

The stance in this dialogue is defensive. Biologically oriented to uphold regulation and ferret out potential threats, this protect-and-defend cycle attracts unregulated situations that trigger resistance energy.

DISSOLVE THE PAST

THE FREEZE IN FLEEING

Someone in their early twenties is raised in a strict home where they were raised to defer to their parents in every area. After leaving home for some time, they reflect on their awkwardness around others, their fear of being publicly asked their opinion, and their indecisiveness on menial affairs. Privately, they fear being put on the spot.

I don't like being asked my opinion. What if it's the wrong one? What if I offend someone and they don't like me? I don't want people knowing about the way I was raised, who my parents are, or the fact that I didn't have the same experiences they all seem to share. Why was I raised this way?

This person has premeditated a series of evasive scripts in order not to be exposed for the imposter they feel they are. This vigilance to position themselves at the fringe of attention is the triggering of flight.

Each example begs the following question. *If someone is that aware of the problems that cause them the greatest pain, then why don't they change?*

Though most of us can express our worst traits better than other people can, we didn't develop our worst traits by *thinking* about them. We developed them by generating a tremendous amount of neurological energy that locked them into our biological systems.

Because it's neurological energy that got us there, it must be the release of neurological energy that will discharge the freeze. In other words, *homeostasis.*

In the same way you can't walk across a room using psychological energy, you can't change behavior that way either.

Robbie Grayson III

A Personal Story

I was a bedwetter right out of diapers until almost age eleven. Even when the cost of wetting the bed was greater than the embarrassment I feared for wetting the bed, I still didn't manage to control my bladder. Over time, I learned to hide the evidence, although badly. And when the evidence was discovered, I resorted outright to denying it, even in the face of more punishment.

A few years ago when speaking to my father, I learned something about him that I don't recall ever having heard before. He had joined the Air Force right out of high school at age seventeen. I remember him as a severe man who resembled a drill instructor. At a young age, he taught me to make my bed military style with hospital corners on both ends and sides and the top cover tucked in so tightly that he could bounce a quarter off it. He taught me how to shine my shoes until they gleamed. He taught me to iron my clothes along the seams, perfectly, using enough starch that they could resist a day of wrinkling.

All of this discipline, however, I learned in a high-stress environment—as if life depended on it. Back to my story.

Because my father was a minor at the time he wanted to join the military, my grandmother had to give her permission for him to join. I had heard that before. But what I learned in this conversation that I hadn't heard before was that his *first* choice was the United States Marines. My grandmother wouldn't sign him up for the Marines, but she would sign him up for the Air Force. So, my father took his second choice, which was the Air Force.

I wasn't sure at the time why that new information shocked me, but it did. When I later shared it with a friend, his words startled me even further.

"You were raised by a Marine."

That night, at almost forty-seven years of age, I had an "accident."

I awoke confused until I realized that I had wet myself. When I investigated further, I realized that I had wet myself but hadn't wet the bed. After changing and getting back into bed, I awoke the next morning, wondering if it really had happened. When I found my wet clothes in the washing machine, it dawned on me. What my parents had tried to teach me as a child for so many years, I had never been able to do until that moment, which was *when I felt the need to use the restroom at night, wake up and go to the bathroom.*

But that *never* happened. I had gone from wetting the bed to no longer wetting my bed without learning the lesson, which was *interrupt the cycle before it begins.* At age forty-seven, I finally completed a developmental step that most children learn by age five or six. And what was that step? *Interrupting a biological cycle.*

Dissolve the Past

Something else happened that made the incident leave me with a lasting impression. I finally was able to make sense of my father's severity towards me as a child and young man: he was a Marine raising Marines. Not only did that new information make me feel strangely calm, but it reinterpreted my childhood through the lens of compassion for my father, who, when prevented from becoming a Marine, *still found a way to become one.*

What psychology couldn't teach me through years of talk therapy, rationalization, blameshifting, and self-loathing, biology made right by my almost wetting the bed—but then interrupting the act.

Dissolve Your Past

A story goes that two monks were walking along a beach when they saw a woman drowning beyond the surf. The elder monk jumped in and saved her. The monks continued on their journey.

After some time had passed, the younger monk lashed out at the elder monk.

"Our religious order says that we aren't supposed to touch women, and you touched one."

The elder monk replied.

"You're still back on the beach, trying to save her."

The lesson is obvious. What the elder monk *did* solved the problem. It saved a life. But what the younger monk *thought* sentenced him to a life of reliving that moment when he didn't save one and psychologically trying to save that woman another way, which we all know can't happen.

Be like the elder monk.

CREDITS

BOOKS

Levine, Peter A. *Waking the Tiger: Healing Trauma: The Innate Capacity to Transform Overwhelming Experiences.* North Atlantic Books (1997). ISBN13: 9781556432330

Polar Bear Shaking https://youtu.be/xDlR-wl7iFI

Scaer, Robert. *The Body Bears the Burden: Trauma, Dissociation, and Disease.* Routledge (2001). ISBN13: 9780789012463

Smith, Huston. *Forgotten Truth: The Common Vision of the World's Religions.* HarperOne (1992). ISBN13: 9780062507877

Tolle, Eckhart. *Stillness Speaks.* New World Library (2003). ISBN: 157731400X

Van der Kolk, Bessel, M.D. *The Body Keeps the Score: Brain, Mind, and Body in the Healing of Trauma.* Penguin Books (2015). ISBN13: 9780143127741

Quotes

p. ix. Richard Carlson. American Author, Psychotherapist & Motivational Speaker | *The past isn't comparative. It can't be worse or better than it was.*

p. 27. Eckhart Tolle. German-born Spiritual Teacher & Self-help Author | *Stress doesn't care about now. It cares about later, which is a want that can never be granted.*

p. 41. Marcus Aurelius. Author of *Meditations* | *You must hush the mind if you are to hear what you must do to survive.*

p. 59. Robert Scaer. Board Certified Neurologist | *Unlike other species, humans must contend with their minds as well as with their bodies.*

p. 77. E.M. Alexander. American Social Media Influencer | *Psychology can't do what behavior can.*

p. 73. Jane Austen. English Novelist | *If we really want to change, we can find a way.*

p. 117. Ram Dass. American Spiritual Teacher | *Denial is what causes suffering.*

TRAITMARKER MEDIA, LLC
www.traitmarkermedia.com
traitmarker@gmail.com

About the Author

Robbie Grayson III is the founder of Traitmarker, Traitmarker Books, and Traitmarker Media, LLC. He lives in Franklin, Tennessee, with his wife and children.

Take the Free Assessment
www.traitmarker.com

Contact the Author
traitmarker@gmail.com

Get the Next Book
www.traitmarkermedia.com

www.ingramcontent.com/pod-product-compliance
Lightning Source LLC
LaVergne TN
LVHW012054070526
838201LV00083B/4719